GW00467568

i

I Like It Cuz It's Pink

Poems

By Sarah McMahon

For my family, who continue to show me unconditional love, who laugh at my oddities, and who always make time to read my poems.

For my friends, who have become a second family. You are loved and appreciated endlessly.

And for all the men who inadvertently taught me to love myself first, and harder.
[Be better.]

Table of Contents

Good Love

Love is a first date that eats up a whole night without indigestion.

The OG Love Poem
(all the rest suck)

~for Preston

if I were to play the victim
I would use a saxophone for Pachelbel's *Canon in D*
that makes no sense, but neither do I
and I hate when he tries to make sense of me
some things are not meant to be quantified, like
> *I love you so much*
> *How much?*
I don't know, you're a 10 out of 10
or a 12 if I'm trying to be clever

he knows me without even trying
laughter has always numbed my pains
but he sees right through me
and laughs anyway
his smile makes me smile
when nothing else will

I just want to sit down so I don't have to fall
but I already have and that feels so insane
my therapist says
insanity's not what plagues me
I've got heart disease caused
by a mother-fucking man
who said he'll always be there,
and meant it

who said *I love you unconditionally*
and never left when I pushed him to leave
who picked up my broken bits
and put them away in a zip lock bag

so I could fix myself when I finally felt safe
who gave me a small golden box
with a small golden bow
and nothing inside
because his heart wouldn't fit

so I placed my right ear
to the left of his chest
put his rhythm to memory
to never forget

I've got heart disease
caused by a mother-fucking man
who understands this poetry-speak
who carved his name in the soles of my feet
so I'll always be able to find him

I have wished
on one million stars
in one million skies
to find a love like this

Vancouver

~For Chuck

city where angels dream
where no one needs saving
where parking is cheap
and mountains are free
where I ripped open my knees
running through trees
over rocks and streams
slipped and fell right into you,
Vancouver
city of long summer days and deep
throaty nights where the highlight reels play
the same marching tune
it is June
and new love makes everything brighter
Vancouver
I want to bottle you up and drink you
today
tomorrow
forever
fall asleep with your taste on the tip of my tongue
I've never met anyone like you
a rooftop pool, a train ride, a mural
enough time to recognize myself deep in your eyes
I gave a homeless man four navel oranges
he said, "God bless you"
and I walked away shaking
Vancouver
you've buried yourself in my skin
you're the city I hoped would exist
a city of pure happiness
with a voice like a cello and hands like
home

you're the sweater I pull over my head
when earth starts to sleep
when winter settles into my everything
you are warmth
and light
and love
Vancouver

to the man in the suit and blue checkered tie

~you know who you are

you caught my eye and you knew it
not normally drawn to someone so dark
not normally drawn to a stranger
you ask me to dance, for some reason I do
ask me to smile so I frown, and you laugh
ask for two shots of tequila, I take one
never intending to enjoy your attention
you ask me upstairs
promise nothing will happen
I consider your offer
run to my room
and deadbolt the door
pretend I can't hear you knocking
turn on the shower to sit in the steam
wonder how the hell I got here
in a Marriott room with swan folded towels
breath mints and bottles of mineral water
feeling so small
for craving attention
one of those pesky, messy
human conditions
when I think of you now
I think of your wife
the agony you must have caused her
or will, whenever she learns
that her man is a child
who won't get lost on his way
to the gingerbread house
will simply consume it
gorge himself on pink lollipops
gumdrops, chocolates, and taffy

7

I hope she knows
that her man is a child
who needs to feel needed
one of those pesky
messy
human conditions

Footsie

~For Benji

I found a foot pimp online

which only means a strange man
offered to sell photos of my feet
and take a portion of my earnings

men always think they can help me

his said his name is Benji
he knows the industry
has a short list of clients just waiting
to hand me a pile of cash

the thing is, Benji, my feet aren't pretty
they are blistered and calloused I'm sure
some people are into that but
you clearly don't know who I am

I've let men walk across my body
like a red carpet, let them tell me
things I wanted to hear like
I love you to death
but my heart's still beating because
no one has meant that yet

I've watched men earn more money
than me for jobs they do poorly
let them talk over me under me through me
I try not to let them come close
guard my heart with a firehose

but I do know one truth about men

they love compliments lap up praise
like small boys swallowing birthday cake

Benji, I don't need your help selling photos
I don't need anyone to pimp me out
did some online sleuthing and found
more about you though, I know

where you live, how old you are
the license plate on the back of your car
you used to work in finance
have three pet cats
listen to Rush Limbaugh

I know you ache for attention
and here I am giving you a goddamn poem
because I want you to know
you can't scare me
hiding behind your computer screen
threatening me vaguely

real men don't need to sell photos
of feet they can see them in real life
by not being a creep
I hope I meet you someday
so I can shake your hand
look in your eyes and smile
just to see you squirm

in the meantime
I wish you
the sweetest, raunchiest
foot fetish dreams
a pile of cash
and a nice, pretty girl
who loves playing footsie

It's Chess, Darling

~For Zakir

he said, explaining a UFC match on TV
a punch, a jab, an upper cut right to the face
check mate
broken jaws arms that can snap any bone
and fire in their eyes, they
just want to fuck something up

it's chess, darling he said
caressing the back of my neck
leaving indents of steam
where his fingers touched me
felt agonizing want
from the back of my throat
all the way down to my feet

there are monkeys playing handball in my chest
and I'm supposed to maintain my composure
so he'll never know
that I'm hanging off the edge of a crescent moon
too terrified to let go
falling in love is chess, darling
they are all rooks and we are both kings
stuck in a stalemate

if I did admit I loved him
I'm afraid he wouldn't say it back
just like my dad
who taught me that being a man
means letting shame consume you slowly
swallow you like quicksand
means American anger proud and afraid
tears are weakness, goddamnit

taught me love is giving a woman breadcrumbs
so she's always craving more
love means settling, not keeping score out loud
but it's a title match and I've got the endurance
to swing and miss talk some real shit

like a family history of wandering men
a woman who sunk her teeth into five of them
led her baby boy into the shallow dungeons
of hearts not ready to hold him
taught him weak men leave their families behind
so he stayed, battling anger in a winter depression
that bled all over the rest of us

if we ignore the pain it'll go away, right?
like a real tough man, hey dad
the demons swirling around in your belly
will eat you alive if you keep them inside

they swallowed me, too
until I lay in a hospital room
with a tube in my arm, anorexia dancing
across my body like a sore loser
and a doctor looking down on me promising,
if you keep this up hun, your next move is death

I won't forfeit this match if you don't
look shame in the eye and find a mirror
it's chess, darling he said in my ear
smiling like a goddamn magazine cover
glossy and perfect
trying to love me the best way he can
which is to say not like my dad
which is to say I'm tearing apart at the seams
these genes don't fit anymore

I'm a blind woman walking straight into quicksand

trusting his hand can keep me safe
check mate
this body wasn't built to give up easy
hope is just a word we whisper in our sleep
while we wait for our lives to change
I can't limbo anymore
and I'm done keeping score
it's chess, my love
he whispered again
and I let him

Contradictions

~For Zakir

I have an iron but no board
a bugle but no boy to play it
a heart full of love but no good way
to convey it up my throat off my tongue

I've got a toilet but no paper
windows but no drapes
like my space but want you to be closer
always

I don't want to need you, but I do
have too many shoes but no clean socks
boxes of photos and love notes and tchotchkes
a rusty harmonica
I'll never touch to my lips
I've got the hips of a woman
the awe of a child
and the depth of a tomb

enough time to write you this poem
to let you know
I miss you

I've got an Easter bunny window cling
curling slowly off the glass
but the season's long past
I'm just waiting to see how long it can hold
how much time will pass before you let me go
like most men do

I've got a raging sweet tooth
but nothing to placate this craving

this is all just a poor way of saying
we are terrifying
and lovely and rare

I can't care about anything
when you're in the room
I let myself swoon out the door
float above clouds
scream out loud
I'm in like with you

got a bird's eye view
up here in this swoon
and it might be too soon
but I think
I mean love

Golden Lions

~For Me

we condemn the destruction of empires
golden lions munching on
hummingbirds
a healthy, beating love of self
we pray for salvation to t-shaped logs
pointed   up   up   up
to a freckling sky

I know it is wrong to not notice sunrise
fall asleep to men heavily treading my body
let them explode slowly inside me
I ache to be clean as freshly bleached sheets

I know it is wrong
to recognize pain and do nothing about it
it is not love
to be held and adored like a fuckable puppy
if I were a man
I'd feel no guilt for my body
no loathing for wanting someone to hold me
no hatred of mirrors, no lusting for bones
I'd know how to speak and be heard
how to self-aggrandize

not think of my wrinkling skin
not pay for silicon-injected lips
bigger tits, curvy hips, all of this
leaves me vacant and scared of the sun
despising the men who beg me to hush
I will rise from the dust
of my crumpled bed, screaming

if I were a man
I would fear me
a fervent mess of raw womanhood
with fine smile lines
and a voice like an organ

I eat hummingbirds
from the mouths of lions
shout my own name
from the top of Mount Whitney
I am an empire

point my feet to the east
and walk to the sea
with a spear in one hand
and gold round my feet
it is good to leave
smiling sweetly

Letter to My Younger Self, Version I

when your mother bakes you a cake
thank her
eat a piece
do not worry what will happen to your body
nothing will happen to your body

when a boy texts you late at night
do not answer
when a boy you don't like
asks for your number
give him your fathers'

when you learn how to purge
tell no one
when you learn how to purge
turn on the faucet
when you learn how to purge
don't

when your grandmother calls
answer the phone
when you walk by a homeless girl
stop
give her a sandwich

when a man you're in love with calls you a bitch
go home
when a man you're in love with calls you a cunt
go home
when a man you're in love with leaves bruises
throw his things out a window
lock doors
do not answer his phone calls
do not answer

when your dog dies, keep her name tag
tie it around your neck
when you learn how to eat again, eat
tattoo a lotus on your bicep to celebrate life
when someone asks what it means, say
I almost died, but I didn't
just to see their surprise

when you cancel your wedding
be thankful you avoided more bruises
when you write, be so truthful it hurts
when you sing, be so joyful it burns
when you laugh, do not try to quiet yourself
when your therapist says
you don't need me
say *yes, I do*

when a married man asks you to dinner
say no
when you download Tinder,
delete it
you don't need it

when your doctor finds cancer
do not cry
do not shake
when your mother offers to fly
2,000 miles to hold your hand
as they cut it away
let her

when your mother says
I love you
believe her
say it back

Bad Love

there is no user guide
for how to gently break a heart
how to hold it beating
without squeezing too hard

I like it cuz it's pink

cotton candy   bubblegum   roses   and rosé
flamingos   grapefruit   lollipops
half-washed blood stains
on a pale pink thong
my lips   his lips   her lips   kisses
pink panther   Pink Floyd   pretty in pink
Valentine's Day heart-shaped declarations of
luv u 4ever babe bmine

I like it cuz it's pink he said between my legs
like a good boy
kissing it licking it flicking it
none of it felt great but I also didn't hate it
liked the way his mouth tasted after we finished
pink eyes   pink lies   the pink t-shirt I was wearing
when he promised me
I will love you forever

the way his mouth quivered
the way my spine shivered
the way I learned words
don't mean a damn thing

there's a rare pink river dolphin in South America
endangered by humans dumping shit in our water
opening our mouths and closing our eyes
surprised when we see something gorgeous
surprised that anything we do
could lead to our demise

I like it cuz it's pink
I whispered in his ear
the Christmas he bought me a beryl stone necklace

23

shaped like an *S* for my name
he thought I'd adore some narcissistic jewelry
and I do, or I did before I threw it in the river
after he left, stomped on me
like a pink starburst wrapper
stuck to the sole of a shoe
spit chewed and swallowed
like a stork swallows fish
whole and squirming all the way down

he promised if I jumped high enough
and dove into him
I'd find a rare pink river dolphin
swimming in his chest
I like it cuz it's red
he whispered the night
he carved out my heart and bit it
his lips turning pinkish like they always did
when I kissed him with lipstick

pink matter   pink salt   pink lemonade
pretty in pink Valentine's day heart-shaped
declarations of *luv u 4ever babe bmine*

One Too Many Dick Pics

~For Derrick

one, is one too many dick pics
hey baby sweetie pie sugar plum
I've got a present for ya

really? a Tiffany bracelet?
a check for rent? front row
seats at a Laker's game?
a dotted line
where I sign my name
and take yours?
wait

a dick pic is not a gift
it's an ego boost
a power move
the best and worst thing about you
is your dick
your obsession with it

man, it's not even big
maybe four or five inches
on a generous day, are you in?
(oh, you're *done)*

the only one impressed
by your dick is you, oughta go
on a honeymoon with your schlong
I've known all along
you've got an ego bigger than
the playboy mansion, boy
you've got balls, I'll give you that
but I'm not sending you

a photo back
I'll keep my tits wrapped
and my pants zipped high
no doesn't feel great does it?
but at least you asked
you never gave me the chance
to not see this photo

you, and him, and he should know
that one
is one too many dick pics

Just Another Breakup Poem

~For Derrick

I have no heart for the men who consume me
tear open my chest cavity, let cockroaches seep
from my veins stack themselves
like library books beneath my bed and scream

I can't stand to sleep

don't know how to feel
in your presence or absence

another man offered to buy me diamonds
maxi dresses strappy high-heeled sandals
but he can't make me laugh like you can

I know you're not a maintenance man
your job is not to shove putty in my cracks
stabilize my foundation
help me feel a bit less crazy

I had a dream I died beneath
an avalanche of Allen wrenches
and didn't even scream
because I knew you wouldn't hear me

we are tactile creatures
but no one ever teaches us
how to love another person
expecting nothing in return
there is no user guide
for how to gently break a heart
how to hold it beating
without squeezing too hard

I love you

but never knew how to say it
thought to write it on a gum wrapper
slip it in your pocket for you to find
after you told me goodbye
thought maybe I should call you
so I wouldn't have to look in your eyes
thought I'd better write a poem
it's the best way I know to be honest

I don't want my scars
to bleed onto you and leave bruises
no one ever teaches us what to do with pain
so we give it away
or bury it deep, convince ourselves
we don't need anything
like true fucking fools
like a court jester cackling madly
to please a purple queen

you don't need to say anything

I will sew my eyes closed with pink ribbon
so I won't have to watch myself miss you
cover lips with Lidocaine to forget
how right it felt to kiss you
I deleted all your photos but your image
is engraved in the front of my brain
I need space
to feel angry, hurt, and sad
last night I went to yoga class
sat on my mat and sobbed up my lungs
for you, for me, for us

Beverly Hills

~For Zakir

in Beverly Hills
restaurants leave water dishes outside for dogs
offer them complimentary biscuits
while hundreds of people sleep on the street
life's not fair says everybody
but it doesn't have to be so extreme

in Beverly Hills
I fell in love with a man with large brown eyes
and a smile that unties his whole face
he promised not to hurt me
the first red flag I chose to ignore
now I've collected enough
to sew a king-sized blanket
eight inches thick

in Beverly Hills
there is a clock repair shop that fixes dead watches
he emphasized his lack of time
his clock face stuck on not enough
there are clean white department stores
dripping in diamonds, fur-lined black holes
we disappeared inside
money can't buy happiness
but it can buy a pair of Balenciaga sneakers
and Rolex watches security cameras
in case someone knocks, God forbid
we keep our doors locked

in Beverly Hills
there are tarpits where dire wolves
and saber-toothed tiger bones

bubble up from the depths of the earth
we puzzle their bones back together again
like I puzzle my heart back in my chest
button it up with iron clamps to close it tight
in case he comes back

in Beverly Hills
there is a man who sits on a wide white couch
folding his laundry and scrubbing his hands
he can see germs crawl up his arms
consume his skin
I can't help but feel like I'm one of them

there are mansions and gardens and
hipsters drinking kombucha beer
I don't feel at home here, on the streets
in the mansions
in the arms of a man
who dispassionately kisses my cheek
leaves me craving a taste I can't yet name

there are palm trees blinking at the setting sun
a man full of fire and broken love
I thought I could change, a fool's game
rolling dice down Rodeo Drive
hoping to turn a quick buck
I've run out of luck and this town
is a bad storybook ending
shattered glass slippers
frogs that don't turn into princes
kisses that can't wake me up

in Beverly Hills
there are clovers
peeking through sidewalk cracks
a man left wondering where I am
folding his laundry
and washing his hands

Operation

Adam's Apple
bobbed up and down as he spoke and caught my eyes like a worm on
a fly-fishing rod, "this is pretty damn strange," I thought.

Wishbone
saved from Thanksgiving turkey we pulled apart to see who would get
the bigger piece which meant a year of blessings, but I never yanked
hard enough who knew love would require the pulling apart the
mending, the scars.

Broken Heart
I felt it coming before he said *let's be friends* before he busted my
chest open and shocked me to death before he sunk his teeth in my
aorta and squeezed, his beautiful mouth sucking life out of me, how
he stared at my tears as if he'd never seen water and touched them in
wonder.

Funny Bones
aren't good at telling jokes, remind us we're human when we bring in
the groceries, bump into doorframes and wince. These days, it takes
two trips.

Spare Rib
the one I gave to him so we could be less of an "I" and more of an
"us" how he never asked me too, it's just what I thought I was
supposed to do.

Butterflies in Stomach
on our first date he wore a suit and looked hard in my eyes without
flinching, which made me want to cry which made me realize how
fucked up I am. And the butterflies danced.

Breadbasket
a funny way to say "stomach," home of the butterflies. Empty the day, night, morning, month after he told me goodbye.

Writer's Cramp
this act of purging makes me love myself completely. The keyboard sounds like rain and my fingertips are numb, proving to myself I don't need anyone.

Charlie Horse
that nagging pain from laughing too hard tangled in bed when nothing mattered but his skin on my skin. If I close my eyes tight enough, I can still smell him.

Water in the Knee
a funny way to say age is just a number, until it turns around and drags you into a doctors' waiting room, next to a happy, pregnant couple, a funny way to be metaphorically slapped in the face.

Anklebone Connected to the Knee Bone
songs we sang as children, bubbling up to bite our extra flesh, to remind us we're nothing special, all just ligaments and tendons, bones and sour words we can't take back, apologies fall flat, don't they?

Wrenched Ankle
an ankle sprain can heal completely in six, tiny weeks I only wish the same were true for me it's taken a lifetime to assemble myself messily cut open scarred over and bleeding again for as long as I'll let myself bleed.

No operation can piece me together, see?

Anxious Avoidant Attachment

~For Scott

your avoidant behaviors
are activating my anxious reactions

like a pinball machine
like the Operation man
when you touch the edge of his chest
where his heart ought to be
the metal edges electrocuting

I wish he would scream

I want to write a thank you card
to everyone on earth who has hurt me
I don't want that to be you
but I'll write you one, too

I am a heroin addict
chasing the same high I felt the first night
your body wove into mine

I feel a bit crazy
like an unhappy lady in a sitcom
whose friends always tell her
to run from the man
they know will hurt her
but she doesn't
cuz then there wouldn't be a show
and the viewers roll our eyes
we know it ends
we've seen it a million times
but Karen gives Brad

another chance
another chance
another chance
and before she knows it
she's built her life around a man
before she knows it
she doesn't understand who she *is* anymore

I don't want to be Karen
and I don't want you to be Brad
but I'm a rubber band, just about to snap
it's not difficult, really

I need a man who is alpha enough
to be able to trust
who can hold my heart without squeezing too hard
who isn't afraid of maybe just
maybe us not working out
who wears his heart on his sleeve, you could say
but that's a cliché
and clichés are the dumbest fucking things
writers fall prey to

like I might fall prey to you
if I didn't know better

I am part wolf, part double X
chromosome
will protect myself
and my young and my mate
from all the hatred and terror
and fucked up shit in this life

every night before I close my eyes
I check the doors and windows
make sure I've locked down the hatchets
sleep with a gun at the foot of my bed
and one under my head, just in case

I need to feel safe

but I'm walking on bloody eggshells
and this life is a white carpet

if you earn my love
you will never be able to drink it all up
it is endless

and there is no one like me
there will be dozens of people
you could build a life with
some pretty young thing
with blonde hair and blue eyes
who might not be as intense
and you might think she's a 10/10
but no number is big enough to define
how much I'm able to love

whatever happens, hun
remember me
I'll remember you
and I'll love you too
from a distance
if I must

it's not difficult, really
to be alpha enough
to be able to trust your instincts
mine are screaming at me
honey, don't you dare
give your heart away
to one more man
who doesn't care

Pros vs. Cons

~For Chase

I already know the pros won't win,
like pros ought to do
If I asked LeBron James for a game
he would flatten me like a gnat on
the windshield of a greyhound bus
now there's an idea—a greyhound bus
where no one can shower, and no one can piss
but they're all going somewhere other than this
my "this" is a 3-foot by 3-foot square wooden table
we bought at Ikea when we still loved each other
a ginger-pear candle sits silent and cold
like the space in between our pillows each night
where the cat used to sleep before finding
more rest under the bed

a pro might be that he loved me so much
he drilled a hole in my chest
stuck his hands inside to squeeze out my love
and drink it, his lips turning pinkish
like they always did when I kissed him with lipstick
a con might be that the hole is still there
and I've not found a filler
ice cream, chardonnay, edibles, blow
I climbed up a mountain and cried my way
down
searching for pros
like a mother hen searches for eggs
she can't understand have been taken
I am sure a hen can feel sadness—*that*
is the empathy I craved so strongly
from not only him, but all men
come inside me, make me feel sexy

make me not want to hide

even poetry is grounded in truth and reality
"is this poem about me?" he once said,
as I tapped out a love poem while sitting in bed
"no, it's a poem about me" I replied
I need my own words to fill my gaping chest hole
I have found the right sounds
they curl on my tongue
like cartwheeling children
my voice resurrected
I cannot forget the strength
of his hands round my wrists
round my neck
how he screamed
you fucking dumb bitch
you're such a goddamn cunt
I don't think my heart-hole can ever unhear this

a con might be that I feel so deeply
a real dumb bitch could never be hurt
by dumb fucking words
would forgive the eight shots of tequila
take him home, go to bed and forget
I feel no strength in forgiving him
that's a con *and* a pro
I know it is healthy
to tally my reasons like this
one for me, one for him, one for us
all for nothing, it seems
but this poem

Men Are Trash

a woman on a talk show said "men are trash"
and the audience laughed
but I just felt bad
had a sour taste in my mouth
wanted to eat her words and spit them out

I had made the same joke
in the aftermath
of the bloodbath
of a breakup
when I couldn't wear make up
without crying it off
when men told me yes, but meant no
told me to grow a spine
or recoiled when I cried

men are trash, dumpster fires
idiotic even when they're just platonic
so ignorant they never think
can't remember birthdays
or four-month two-week
five-day anniversaries

we say men are trash
and can't take it back
words only matter when statements like that
fall upon the ears of a daughter and son
one learns he is not good enough
the other that she shouldn't trust anyone

and I thought about the men I've let love me
drug me with words like
I love you to death

but my heart's still beating
cuz no one has meant that yet

I thought about the men I've regretted
who let me open their wounds and infect them
left them with band-aids
and made up stories
why we'd never last
excuses falling dank and flat

I thought about the men who raised me
praised me when I didn't deserve it
taught me to be fearless
to demand respect
to watch out for the kinds of men
who are trash

who laugh at the cracks in my armor
pour lighter fluid into their mouths
so they sound like a steam engine
a speed demon
the men who idolize demons
march across town
with their guards down
in white robes they know
nobody will harm them

the men who were born
with a twisted blade of hate
hot in their chests
daddy knows best
but daddy's not well

the men who bleed uncontrollably
cover scars with more scars
until their skin is so thick
there's no getting in

and I thought of the man who knelt on a knee
and promised to be the best thing
that would ever happen to me

how he filled me with doubt
tore me down to my bones
nobody knows
the cold words we exchanged
the pain of his fists
bruises
and wishing for any life other than this
when I finally left
I became my own hero
it would be so simple to call him trash
but that's not a story
I could ever take back

he was born with a twisted blade
of hate hot in his chest
daddy knows best
but daddy's not well
and his daddy had secrets
that he'll never tell
shame and guilt and scars
so thick his skin became leather
we should want to be better

a woman on a talk show said "men are trash"
and the audience laughed
but I just felt bad
had a sour taste in my mouth
wanted to eat her words and spit them out

I had made the same joke
in the aftermath
of the bloodbath
of a breakup
when I couldn't wake up

without shaking
couldn't fall asleep without pills
yellow green purple blue
to match my skin
we should want our sons
to be better than this

Pity the Fool

who plants her seeds in a field of concrete
only to reap a bundle of weeds
who cut open her ribcage to watch her heartbeat
only to bleed uncontrollably
who believed
if she were careful to tread softly
into the mouth of the cave
where the grizzly bear sleeps
she might fail to wake him
lie down beside him
hold him and love him hard enough
he might shed his fur
might fail to consume her
pity the fool
who thinks she can change the man
who clawed open her chest,
bit a chunk from her heart only to find
the flavor was bland
pity the man
who ran from love when he had it
who hid in a cave, bitter and angry
dug a deep hole to cover his hurt
and buried himself alive
pity the fool
who plants her seeds in an ocean and cries
when they fail to produce something worthwhile
who walks back to the cave day after day
hoping the bear
will have something to say
pity the fool
who wraps himself in solitude
to hide and rage and laugh
at those who dare
come close

Minor Things

my therapist keeps a 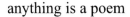pink orchid
in a brown cement pot beneath her window
she turns it sometimes,
so it grows toward the sun
all flowers in time bend toward the sun
I have coasters that read
don't fuck up the table
the best way not to fuck up
is to not give up

anything is a poem

how you curled my name
round the tip of your tongue
blew smoke rings
out the top of a black SUV
I felt like a queen
wore black the day after
you told me goodbye

there is more than one way to lose a person

I will never forget
how you held my head
and gazed in my eyes
I was raw and lovely
your hands made me putty

now our memories ooze
out the back of my mind
there is more than one way
to life a life, just like
there is more than one way
to say goodbye

Dear Reader,

you are likely tired
of reading poems
about heartache and sex
tattered relationships
this mess of a life
but you must realize
we've all been broken
once or twice

Dear Reader

I don't know you
but I know that I love you
isn't that pleasant
and weird and profound?
I hope you've had a nice Sunday
or Monday
Wednesday
or Tuesday
I hope you come to this poem
with an open heart
let me in so I can whisper
I adore you
and mean it
I hope you believe it

46

Self-Love

Alone is a place I always feel safe.

Clearly

If I saw myself clearly, I'd hate myself less

I can make aching, beautiful music with words
make grown men fall to their knees
make the tick-tock of my grandfather clock
match the beat of my heart

if I saw myself clearly
perhaps I could see the woman who makes men
fall to their knees, the woman
so easy to love so hard to please
there are holes in my skin
shaped like a mockingbird
watch me purge, watch me tear up my skin
with dull kitchen scissors

the world is a tragedy to those who feel
but a comedy to those who think

there are weeds between cracks
in a brick sidewalk where a homeless man pees
today, those weeds are stronger than me
I will take a long bath because a magazine
said it would help me feel loved
do a kind gesture buy myself flowers
drink artisanal coffee beneath a yellow umbrella
watch pedestrians pass as they smile and laugh

comparison is the thief of joy

buy 1,000 count Egyptian sheets whiter than bone
drill holes in my fists and color them red
just to feel something
cry orange and green tears smear my makeup

take pictures to prove that nothing is real
make a milkshake and give it away
to the homeless man peeing on weeds

beggars can't be choosers but
if he asked for a dollar I'd give him two

we are mad contradictions
each moment is here and then gone and the hands
of my grandfather clock spin relentlessly
piercing the air til it bleeds red like my sheets
my thumbs turn to plums in a lukewarm bath
rub my eyes and they leak orange and green

when I see myself clearly, I hate myself less
make aching, beautiful music with words
and fall to my knees

This Woman

sad small lonely *spiteful* woman
heartsick   lovesick   feverish   woman
woman alone, what is wrong with this woman?

soft smiling simple savage woman, with
too many crew necks and not enough cleavage
too many letters behind her name
scaring the *sad small* men away

once upon a time
a daughter was born
and lived and died
without the burden of a   man-child
the hurdle of a   man-child
the ass-wiping
ankle-biting
headache of a   man-child

and when she was laid
in a *shallow* grave
a *stranger sighed,*
"*sad small* lonely *spiteful* woman
could never find her a man, poor woman"

what a *strange seductive sinful* woman
no hankering for children, woman
ought to push *small* humans from her loins
snap her *spine* in half
put life on hold, grow old for children
what is wrong with this woman?

this *snarky sorry soulful* woman
who *spends* days writing poems

50

nights in a pub with hungry men
who wonder aloud
"why haven't you *settled* down yet, woman?
you'd make a *sharp* wife, any man
would be lucky to have you, woman"

silly sardonic smiling woman
who *shall* not be had by a man
who *sinks* her teeth in a *side* of raw beef
cuz she likes how it feels
to crunch bones in her teeth

who *shines* like a mother-fucking galaxy
her dreams are brighter than *suns*
bolder than anything or anyone

she etches a *scarlet S* on her chest
for *sad small* lonely *spiteful* woman
strong sharp saucy satisfied woman
sensuous spiritual sparkling woman
this woman

Truth Is

~For Kiki

I feel stale in my skin
like a saltine cracker
that sits in the cupboard gathering dust
Sylvia Plath stuck her head in an oven to die
I only fantasize about being warm
heat rises and dust settles
I fear settling
the green, acid ghost
of stagnant fear punches my throat
expectations are the root of all disappointment
like a waitress serving you
soggy French fries or stale French toast
the French like to dress all in black,
they are regal
as painted dogs or fine china
or *Elle* magazine
I don't know anything
color my face to feel pretty (not *be*)
wake up drunk from cheap vodka
watch TV shows of home makeovers
a kitchen sink overflows
the pit of a date is stuck in the drain
the maintence man frowns
says sinks are not meant to swallow seeds
I watch a pastor swallow a wafer
he wants me to donate my savings
to heavy collections plates
so he can buy a private airplane
life is a disaster
or, an adventure
there is no reason to sing

happy days are here again
on congested street corners
streak naked in front of the louvre
make art out of nothing
make life out of art
I met a new friend who took my picture
and colored it neon
while I sat beside her
writing this poem
we weren't in an oven but
I've never been warmer

Confessions

Forgive me Father for I have sinned

plucked stickers from standard apples
and used them to buy organic
I don't want to die. *Why*
do you go by "Father?"

You must have a name,
Bernie or Chuck or William or Sam
Sam's a nice, non-gendered name.
When I think of Sam, I think of a girl
with bright red hair in two long braids
nearly down to her waist,
I think of my best friend's Jewish fiancé
that kid's book called *All About Sam.*

I'm glad my mother read to me, glad
I learned to read so I can see your degree
"Mr. Matthew Brady, MBA"

what made you change your mind?
in another life I might have fucked you

forgive me Father, for I have sinned

but it's not really me, it's this pesky flesh
these eyes make men feel so alive
this brain, this face, this body, this mind

hail Mary, full of grace
I bought a few organic apples
for the low, low price of $1.99

54

I don't want to die

do you ever go by *"Daddy?"*
sometimes men like to hear that in bed
like me to whisper hot noise in their ears
like me to moan and writhe
scratch and scream you might blame *them*
for how they touch *me*
how their fingers linger high on my hips
in each notch of my spine
how I shiver in pleasure

it's this pesky flesh
these impossible standards
the virgin mother is a pregnant nightmare
I wake to relief in bloody sheets

Father, forgive me for being so bold
but I don't think your manhood
can understand me
I don't want your blessing
I want you to see
the apple core lodged in your cheek

Old Souls

I've been told I have an old soul
it's been roaming the Earth for centuries
I am only the latest vessel

I have no date of birth, no birth mark
beneath my rib cage branding me human

a soul predates the modern calendar
the modern inclination to measure all we do
in seconds minutes hours
neatly parsed and parceled
shipped the day before Christmas
with no return address
expected to arrive safely and on time

expectations are the root of all disappointment

I never expected anyone to love me
so nobody did, or I didn't believe them

believing in love is like believing in God
we hope he exists, hope there is more
to this green and blue ball in an endless black sky
than to live and to die and to rot in the ground
in a box picked out by a widow
or daughter or great-aunt's niece
choosing a coffin is a feminine task
women live longer, and men have no foresight
for things so predictable as their own demise

I have found Easter eggs in July
made cranberry sauce in June
rolled naked in sand in mid-January
to usurp the predictable

I have an old soul
that nobody knows how to label
sidewalk chalk washes away at the sign of rain
permanent markers, ink pens, irons in fires
nothing on earth is forever
even the stars will burn up and fade
but this soul has been floating
through bodies and minds
for a long, long time

at the end of my body
when my niece picks a coffin
I hope it is blue like the ocean
and soft like the sky
imagine the lives that have lived in
this soul
we are not old, but a continuation
of air and water
breath and life
and sweet, precious
relentless
time

Hey, Brain

Don't you want me to *gleam* like
those bitches in *Shape* magazine?
asses tits abs and ribs headlines that scream:

Get Your **BEST Butt EVER**!
Bikini Body in **2 Weeks** Flat!
Look Great **Naked**
Slim & Happy
Firm & Fit
Unleash Your Inner **SEX Goddess**
Shredded Abs in 5!

My therapist said I should unsubscribe
but I can't
let go of the thigh-gaps
make-up hacks
clean recipes
I can't
let go of glossy pages
promising beauty at any age
the male gaze
the lists of tricks and tips and ways
to make myself pretty
I can't
understand how
I can't
understand my own brain.

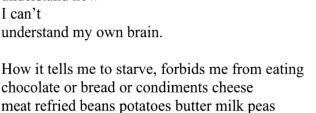

How it tells me to starve, forbids me from eating
chocolate or bread or condiments cheese
meat refried beans potatoes butter milk peas
anything sweet, how can my brain
know better than me?

Convince my eyes my reflection is tepid,
unflattering

Hey, Brain

I would like you to take
a back seat for a while
I am the driver and Pavlov was right
I can condition you not to believe in yourself
you did it to me

and I'll hide
the bare asses in magazines
until I can see the photoshop
glaring back at me

Hey, Brain

I need you to wait
until I figure this out
then we can be friends again but for now
it's best that we take a long break
maybe move far away until I feel safe

Hey, Brain.

Cool Girls

~For all of us

cool girls can hang
we laugh at dick picks
throw back shots of jaeger
without making a face
we're not into PDA
but take it hard from behind
know just the right moment to moan like
ahhhhh
cool girls like being alone but
morph into a social butterfly
anytime you want
watch football and act like we care
eat burgers or steak or lobster or snails
cool girls don't ever let on
when something is wrong
we bury that shit deep
the stuffing of a teddy bear
bursting at seams but we never explode
go blow off some steam at the gym
lululemon
we dress to impress without trying too hard
don't spend too much time on our phones
not concerned with appearances, but
she's fucking hot, bro
cool girls don't make too much noise
take up too much space
never roll our eyes at a catcall
never raise our voice
when
he follows us home
just

speed up our steps
break
into a run
cool girls should know better
than to walk home alone
cool girls *hush*
we don't want to cause problems
never cry wolf
(never cry)
we take care of ourselves
got backbones of stone
stiff enough to keep us upright
wound just tight enough to be crazy fun
but not too crazy
we don't expect much
if you lie cheat or hurt us
we'll let you off easy
breezy
cool girls

Binge & Purge

a new therapist wants me to play
the same, tired game
dig up my past and kill it again
air it all out just to bury it deep
we are gathered here today
to say different words
that mean the same thing

I was Anorexic
Bulimic
I pinged and purged
now consume words
and throw up on paper
splatter paint style

I dated a boy
who wanted so badly to be a man
but he had too much rage
so he planted pine trees
trimmed hedges
mowed lawns and pulled weeds
but no water came so he shriveled in sun
I can't love anyone
if I don't love myself
that could be a t-shirt, or an excerpt
from a soggy self-help book

it shouldn't be hard to chew then swallow
resist the urge to run to the toilet
let sour guilt escape down the drain
there is no greater pain
than loving someone
who can't love you back
who isn't equipped to untie his own shoes

one fist is a hammer and one is a wrench

I would tell my younger self
when his tongue is a knife
and your heart the target
you need to run, buy a gun
value yourself more than anyone else
life is too short to waste
dumping guts down a drain
too sweet to spend drowning in gin
too precious to swing on a stalled Ferris wheel
looking down on a jubilant, madding crowd
no one can see their own painted cheeks
cracked skin chipping with sideway grins

I cannot convey all of this
in a 30-minute session
with a woman who sits with pursed, red lips
and nods three times in every direction
how lovely and horrid and grey it must feel
to eat three square meals in a beige brick
home with a glass front door
and pots of cilantro in square windowsills
how can I ask her to shut the fuck up,
I don't want her pity don't need her to fix me
just want her to listen
to help me make sense of my monkey brain
assure me, one day
I won't think about purging
won't need to binge
one day I will wake
to the rupturing sun
and not want to scream
not want anything

Letter to My Younger Self, Version II

stand up straight, girl
stand tall
don't close up your heart like that
don't let that fire burn out
fall asleep to the sound of your own pounding heart
don't ever think a lover can fix you, girl
you won't ever need that kind of fixing
make a list of things you adore
and put yourself first:
you, the moon, strawberry jam
holding hands, music and dancing
and people who don't shy away
don't shy away from yourself, girl
wrap ribbons around your own neck
zip your own dress
don't let anyone take the spring from your step
collect butterflies and swallow them whole
don't ever let go of the girl inside your own veins
who believed in magical kingdoms far far away
where the hurt couldn't get to her, girl
do not look away from those who condemn you
look up and say, *I am a kingdom*
and when the urge to run scratches
the back of your throat, have a cough drop
stand up and swallow your pride
you are nothing and everything at the same time
do not mourn the days you lost hiding
do not be ashamed of nights you spent crying
tears are tiny rivers, and baby girl
nothing is stronger than water
drink it up, but don't let it drown you
I want you to breathe out, hard
when life feels too full

stand up straight, learn to play Für Elise
across keys of your ribcage
and when your Momma says
I love you
I want you to believe her
when your daddy holds your hand
squeeze it tight
do not be afraid of the night
do not be afraid of anything, girl
you can slay monsters
with those piercing blue eyes
you are nothing and everything
at the same time
girl, square those shoulders
stand tall and proud
don't ever let
your fire burn out

Family Love

"Your father doesn't like chicken," she said
so, I learned even food should cater to men.

Country Poor Kids

~For all of us

hand me down t-shirts
dirt on our faces
Daddy don't shave
spends days at a sawmill
a hayfield
a factory that builds motherboards
got our wires crossed, hey
we growin' up poor

country poor kids
eat Pop Tarts for dinner
watch a broken tv with two grey channels
bathe together for warm water
Daddy's gone and we're livin'
with someone else's daughter
we poor

sneak down a dead-end road
where cattails grow high
shoot glass bottles and try not to die
guns are nothin' to us
we shoot rabbits for stew
and squirrels for fun
we don't listen to anyone

run from police, run
from the crazy-eyed man down the street
we learned how to run
how to rise each day with the blossoming sun
sing songs about love and heartache and beer
we are here oh, we poor

we growin' up poor
country poor kids
in church Sunday mornings
we empty our pockets for grace
go home empty-handed
while the preacher-man fondles
the choir boys, hey
we poor
we ain't got a voice

spend rainy days thinkin' bout
what we could be
a doctor
a lawyer
a singer
let dreams soak up our hurt
let the gravel dirt roads run over our toes
we can't leave without money
can't dream without food
in our bellies, damn
we poor

country poor kids gaze at the stars
never reach for them, no
feed chickens mow lawns
buy dollar store clothes
make love with a man from
upstate
who plants a baby, we become
just another single mother
we poor

can't afford daycare
we breathe clean air
and bake our own bread
honor our dead
break backs for minimum wage

tell our babies they ought to be somebody
tell our mothers they never loved us right
search for our fathers til the minute we die
we poor

fall asleep dreamin' and wakin' up poor
pray to God for salvation, we poor
swallow our pride
yes, ma'am no, sir
we got nowhere to go we got nothin'
but the ground beneath us and Jesus above us
and a preacher man thumpin' his chest
amazing grace will save us wretched poor
growin' up poor
livin' poor
dyin'

we once were lost but now we're found
were blind but now we see

All That Glistens

my mother bought a new birdbath
to place beneath the hummingbird feeder
between the two largest hostas
outside the kitchen window
she adds new water each morning and
scrubs it every Sunday so it shines
she says
even birds deserve
the chance to be clean
and she likes to watch orioles
stick thick beaks
through tiny slits
fail to reach the hummingbird nectar
try so hard for what is not theirs
fail, return, and fail again
like so many of us do
I have never told my mother
how comforting it is
that she cares to make the nectar
plant the hostas
clean the birdbath
I suppose I will neglect to
like so many of us do.

Dear Dad,

~With Love

I slept with a stranger last night
he bought me a drink (or two)
and we talked about nothing and everything
and you
"what's your family like?" he asked
so I talked about mom, and brother, the dog
but my dad, I said

my dad looks like Paul Bunyan
with strong gentle arms
hands that can fix broken faucets
air ducts, change my car's oil
and never complain, a simple brain
with room for love but a mouth
that doesn't know how to convey affection
an affinity for talk radio and Hank Williams
the parent I ran to when I wanted a dollar
to visit a friend, to spend weekends
galivanting through cities and towns
that all felt too small, I said, my dad

was the first person I ran too when I won a race
when I fell on my face and needed attention
I never questioned your love but still
find myself searching
for an older man with strong gentle hands
with room to love me and a mouth that can say it
but dad, all they want is my body
and I'm tired of giving
tired of this great, gaping hole in my chest
I can't recollect ever hearing *I love you*
you mean *I love you* when you say

take care or *stay out of trouble*
when you mail me a toolbox or a popcorn machine
but I grew up not knowing how to love me

so, when a man takes me out for a sushi dinner
and whispers "I'm falling in love with you"
I'm inclined to believe him
but I'm not sure what's true
the man I slept with last night
will never call me again
he was 37, with a voice like the ocean
and kind, crinkled eyes
he called me "intoxicating" and smiled like a lion
licking his lips, I'm so tired of this

and I miss you, but never knew how to say it
afraid my words would push you away
I needed to write this
in solid black ink that can't be erased
a permanent, proper, way to say
I love you right back
stay out of trouble, and dad

I know we're both doing the best we can
I've been tallying my aches
in a book beside my bed
craving whiskey, craving sex
awaking empty and exhausted
today, I gave a man a kiss
and he asked me to come home
but I said no

Momma said

city folk
love autumn drives
through the countryside
love
apple orchards and cherry pie
and counting sheep on the road
from the lake house back to the city
love hayrides
and cutting their own Christmas trees
with a handsaw
a cup of hot cocoa and someone
to shake out the extra pine needles
strap it to the tops of their black
SUV's

city folk
love collecting relics
we still use in our kitchen like
the canning machine that belonged
to Great-Grandmomma Nehring
like to drive past the farm
and complain that cows smell
as if their shit doesn't stink
as if they're not
the ones buying burgers
and steaks and cream cheese

city folk, Momma said
might think you are dirty
or laugh at your accent
but you let them know, baby girl,
you, are a warrior
a dirt-slinging
early-rising

strong-handed warrior
you
are an angel born of the earth
not afraid of dirt
not inclined to give up easy
not accustomed to complaining
don't let anyone
take your spirit away

city folk don't know the world like you do
when they walk by in high shoes
with shiny, straight hair
don't glare at them, girl
they aren't worth your time
don't expect them to notice the sunrise
they don't speak your language
can't keep your secrets
won't know what to do
when you howl at the moon
but don't pay them any attention

I know you need to go
spread your fingers wide
soak up life outside this sleepy farm town
but you can always come back
what a blessing is that?
to feel how deeply
your roots are planted
to flourish beneath your own branches
girl
you, are a warrior
an early-rising
tough-loving
strong-handed
warrior

Population 1,164

dead whiskey and cigar smoke
hardwood floors engraved
with the names of past lovers
and hazy dust dancing in neon lights
capture the night in a bottle
and drink it up when you're homesick
the redneck music honkey tonk-ing
through windows dancing shadows
and country nights so silent
guitar chords bop over hillsides
a back-country lullaby sweet enough
to wake the baby, make her cry out in awe
the harmony of boots stomping in rhythm
the desperate joy in our eyes as we hung
suspended for a moment in time
in a song we all know, a magic show
shattered by a drunk, stumbling man
choosing a fight with a window
the ambulance driver knows
this bar by heart and he knows us all
by name no place will ever feel the same
evenings spent commiserating
singing *I've got friends in low, low places*
like that's something to be proud of
and it was

The Hunters

each autumn my father and brother
bundle in orange and walk with their rifles
through forests to climb high in the trees
and wait

some days they come home empty-handed
but on good days
they bring home their prey
solid deer carcasses still warm with life
we would rejoice because deer meant meat
which meant food which meant dinner
was a certainty for a few months at least

I walked by the gun cabinet every day
for eighteen years and fear never
entered by body
guns only harm us
when someone breaks open the cabinet
loads the rifle and shoots, guns
only scare us when we don't need food

the hunters, elbow deep in deer blood
know what it looks like to die
to see life draining slowing from the eyes
of their prey they know what it is to take
and they do so with grace, give thanks
to the bodies they carry on backs
gut and cut open, for eighteen years
I didn't know to be scared

the hunters began with blunt spears and bows
my brother still carries his arrows
through deep, crunching snow to sit in the forest

and watch the earth move, *that's* beautiful

each autumn when the leaves turn gold
and the air grows cold
and earth starts to slumber
I think of the hunters with love
and I think of their prey with adoration
reconciling conflicting emotions
is one of those pesky
messy human conditions

I remember the sun
hanging low over sleeping
cornfields tucked in deep snow
a single deer sweeping her head to look
in my eyes I stopped breathing
so I wouldn't surprise her

the hunters behind me paused too
rifles silently hung over shoulders
as she pranced away, safe
we let that moment sit on our skin for a while
no words can take me back to that breath
but I do know death
is nothing to fear
that's the heart of it, really

each autumn, my father and brother
bundle in orange and walk with their rifles
through forests to climb high in the trees
and wait

Our Town

is peeling apart at the edges
paint, sidewalks, eyes drooping downward
like two Christmas moons

there are four churches, two bars
and one hair salon where Ms. Michelson
trims split ends and sweeps
town gossip into a tin trash can
turn left at the stop sign
past a softball diamond
littered with cigarette butts enough drugs
in the sand to turn us all mad

our town
burns coal and smokes cigars
eats fried chicken twinkies
and Klondike bars
drinks bourbon and beer
we don't like it here
but it's all we know
so we bury our heads in the snow

our town
has been living in the dark
breathing in cobwebs and not breathing out
we sing *God bless America*
stand for the anthem
deny racism like it's gone out of fashion
complain about immigrants
taking jobs we don't want
we are a town of bad luck
blamed on everyone but us

our newspaper is published on Wednesdays
front page news the mother
locked up for abusing her baby
like her mother and her mother and hers
classifieds, taxes, opinion pieces on cutting grass
a high school football team
built of sour rug rats and tattoos
won their first game all year on a field goal
the next day they were town heroes
and they'll talk about that game
until their smiling faces
grace the obituary page
he was a good man, we'll say
etch his name in a tombstone and fade
away
into fields of corn and rye

picture our town in black and white
living slow and easy like real ice cream
the good kind they had at the root beer
stand
before Ron got sick
and the grocery store opened
and business got bad

our town is lapping up death
like the golden mutt granddaddy saved before
Alzheimer's set in and the hospice man came
last Wednesday
the front page of the paper
was a picture of town shot from a plane
each street, each building on display
stubbornly claiming our place

our town won't go down easy
elbow grease is just a term we tuck in
back pockets and throw around loosely
rub some dirt in it, we'll be fine

last time I visited I picked daisies
from the ditches, sat in a church pew
pretended to pray
promised I'd visit again someday
to remember myself
and everyone else
in my town.

My Church

this is dig-to-the-bottom-of-the-coffee-pot work
drink it up and chew the grounds
look around
you're gonna die someday
so am I
and it's terrifying, right?

the preacher-man who baptized me
dropped dead of a brain tumor
rumor said he had a mistress
and the whole damn town ignored it
smiled at his wife in the grocery store
their Christmas cards
had all four of them splayed
across the page
a mother a father two daughters
and a mistress not pictured

but boys will be boys, right?
and the women who raise them
will look away
and the women who marry them
choose to stay

after he died a new preacher arrived
she was anointed in holy water
kind, a big smile, big heart, big arms
the better to hug us all with, but
half the congregation left
fled like sick sheep dodging a lion
my family sat in the third row from the back
singing and swaying *amazing grace how
sweet the sound* let's admit out loud

a woman isn't good enough

I grew up and moved away
but the church aged in place
stained glass collecting dust
collection plates rusting
last Christmas I yanked out my heart
and bit off a piece for my mother
who wanted to lift up her hands and sing
oh, come oh come Emmanuel
pushed a ten-dollar bill in my hand for collections
hoping they'd dust the stained glass
wishing the season would pass
the church makes me sad

I don't know about God, but I know
he's not angry at me for leaving
for having sex, battered relationships
guarding my heart
against the men in church walls
who wait for foundations
to crack and shatter
so they can save us from sins
we didn't commit

I found a Christian in my bank account
squeezing it dry so I gave him my tithe
and now he's a stained-glass winder duster
in this cluster-fuck called life
I'm not afraid of dying
when I lay down at night
more afraid of dreams haunting me
the Sunday school teacher
who breathed down my neck and caressed it
who complimented my developing breasts
who might read this poem someday
and cringe at the word "mother fucker"
not knowing I wrote it for him

the preacher man moaning and wailing
as the holy spirit coursed through his veins
afraid his humanness would show its face
it's all a brigade
we can quit marching anytime
quit this fistfight with ourselves
nobody else
can get to the bottom of our coffee pots
dig up the grounds and swallow us whole

look shame in the face
and it'll disperse
but that's not anything
I learned in my church

The Tow Truck Man

had skinny blue eyes
and a grey ponytail, the kind bikers wear
with a new rubber band every few inches
he squinted at me, said
"how ya reckon you'll get home?"
gave me a hand onto the passenger seat
"no holiday pay," he told me
nodding sideways at a public bus stop
"towed one of those the other day"
and he glanced at my chest
let his eyes linger a second too long
I clenched my fist
no overtime, even on Christmas
his cellphone buzzed with a photo
of a grinning young girl shooting a gun
"that's my kid" he was beaming,
"you know how to shoot?"
"sure do," I lied, and he approved
gave me an **A** with his up-curled lips
"that's the problem with America,
everyone's scared a guns. Schools
ought to teach proper shootin'" he said
I gnawed my inner cheek skin til it bled
and then, I bit harder
for the blood in hallways and playgrounds
for the guns that took daughters like his
who would never grow into a woman like me
whose cars would never break down
who would never clench her fist in a tow truck
at a driver who eyes her sideways
who will never bite her cheek for a free ride home
he told me he used to drive in the derby
gave it up when he broke too many bones

"figured it was just too dangerous,
what with a daughter and all."

Heritage

poor white America
loves 23 & me

I am 10% Irish
22% German
18% Cherokee, and half
Norwegian, I hold onto that
know half what I am
can map out 50% of my family tree
on ancestry.com but here's the messy thing
about poor white America

my father's father was a rough, raging farm boy
who planted a child in a teenaged mother
and abandoned them both when my father was three
that rough farm boy stole half of my history.

When I look at my past
I see a great grandmother
who sang Norwegian lullabies
read me nursery rhymes
bjornen sover bjornen sover
i sit lune hi
she lost her hearing at 33 and
lived 60 years wrapped in silence

I see a mother whose own mother died
of breast cancer, back before medicine
held any answer, her chest
turned black from radiation she spit
faen helvete at nurses and patients
who couldn't understand the foreign words
dripping from her angry tongue
I am from a strong and fiery past

but most days I'm not certain who I am

we are a nation of immigrants and refugees
who scratched and clawed and climbed
our way up out of muck
some of us less lucky than others
now, poor white America wonders
what happened, how did we wind up
in dying coal cities and farm towns
the rest of the world has forgotten about

we look for our history anywhere we can find it
America isn't a heritage, yet
our nation is three generations thick
and our people long for identity
for full family trees
but poor white America has
fractured our edges
unbuttoned our seams
fucked and screamed
and beat each other to death
looking for answers
to questions we haven't asked yet

so we give each other DNA kits for Christmas
add up percentages: I
am 10% Irish
22% German
18% Cherokee
and half Norwegian
I hold onto that
at least I know
half what I am

Feels Like Home

~For Irene

pink flannel sheets hung on the line
while I spun on a tree swing
watching the poplar die
day by day
like everything does

my great grandmother
watched *Days of Our Lives*
with the volume so high
we could hear it outside
her blue mobile home
memories singe my skin
we are flames
burning cold on this hot
heavy earth

my father planted strawberries
to show us how sweet life could be
my mother washed clothing hung sheets
taught me to save spare change
to look at the sky with wonder and awe
there must be a God
or many of them
with a golden ink pen
starring the sky

I'm not sure why
I feel so at home
anywhere on this Earth
perhaps because
we all love the warmth of the sun
ripened strawberries

collecting spare change
to save up and give away
we all know the pain
of losing someone

we are flames
burning cold
on this hot
heavy earth

Bonus Poems

Corporate America

~For the desk jockeys

the board room windows are weeping

the coffee pot steams
whistles
sputters
to a stop like a dying train

we are zombies talking fast stacking
meetings on meetings like a bad club sandwich
that's sat too long in the fridge
we're so goddamn soggy and fine with it
we fucking hate this shit
(but the benefits are worth it)

if I sawed off my arm or
caught lung disease or
had a soft dick, these benefits got me
if I swallowed a screw or
stepped on hot coals
but birth control?
no, we don't cover those

there are cookies in the break room stale
and crumbling like our mental stability
it's Susan's birthday and we all sing
even though she hates it
and her husband just left
and she's trying not to cry
we all look away
God forbid, *feelings*
don't belong in the workplace

there's a mandatory webinar
on how to be a human
- how to avoid harassment
- how to spot a phishing scam
- how get along with others
goddamn

we are zombies in our driving boxes
zombies in our working boxes
zombies in our sleeping boxes
mother fucking zombies

"Sarah, you just don't seem very engaged"
with the business that pays me
a sterile wage to sit pretty and nod
like a painted dog?
to color inside the lines in black and white
to kiss a million ass cheeks, begging
for more money
more money
more money

I've been spending all my cash on
wine, weed, lattes, and hot yoga classes
tv and sex and loud loud music
to drown my screams

the board room windows are weeping

my soul is seeping out my pores
puddling beneath my desk
we're all a goddamn mess
we just can't admit it here
in this steely grey box where
fluorescent blue lights
stain our eyes red

stupid smiles
stuck on our plastic faces
draw the ace of spades
but show me a diamond
I'll forget all of this
once I give up
enough of my life to retire
in the meantime
I'll lie to myself and everyone else
grin like the village idiot and nod
"I love my job"

American Ego

America smells like shit, grease, and shame
looks like a white man
tastes like flint Michigan
sounds like a scream
feels the way a child feels
when they get away with cheating
on a math test
8+9=10, so it seems

in America bigger is better
rich isn't rich enough
and we can "tough it out" through anything
mislabeling our history books
skewing facts
pull yourself up by your bootstraps
stand for the anthem
or kneel, fuck the system

the American dream is a diet
of ice cream and whiskey
and pills to negate the sugar and booze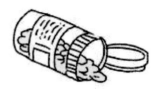
our doctors are tied up in opioids
politicians are stuffed full of lies
Jeffery Epstein hung himself
they say
they say
they say

America is the laughingstock
of the globe and we know it
but relish in it
hang photos of old white men on classroom walls
so children know success when they see it
know authority

what a time to be alive
there's a family drinking insecticide
riots in streets
America is blistering
raw and ragged
angry and tired
of waking up at night in cold sweats
wondering if this is the final
deadly train wreck

we love to feel patriotic but often
don't know what that means
feel a lump in our throats
for the women and men who took an oath
to protect us, meanwhile
kick a kid off a bus for his skin
deny racism
die, due to racism
and the world explodes in opinions
words only matter
when somebody listens

America is a little white lie
that has spiraled into an ocean
the size of our infinite ego
we will bend ourselves over
choke on our pride
until enough of us riot
or enough of us die
or enough of us shut the fuck up
and admit we don't know a damn thing

maybe the problem starts at the top
but we can be the Jenga block
that topples the tower from
the bottom up
if we want.

this quarantine will be the death of me, I think
or at least that's what my brain tells me

I want to sing and dance
paint and read

write poetry until my fingers bleed
but my brain is a marching band
each instrument plays a different song
and I'm supposed to sing along to all of them

in my brain
there is one loaf of bread
at the grocery store and we need
more
more
more

I hoard my food but can't eat anything
my brain is a telephone that won't stop ringing
a broken snooze button
a train horn
a dog whistle
a white noise machine
with the volume turned up so loudly
my floorboards shudder and shake

in my brain
there is an earthquake dismantling
years of therapy
a bookshelf heaving
Jane Austen splayed open
to the page where Mr. Knightley says
"badly done, Emma!"

badly done, brain

this quarantine will be the life of me

I will sing and dance
paint and read
write poetry
until my wounds scab over
and heal completely

in my brain it is spring
windows are open
and fear has faded into grey, grey clouds
raining down on our city
our faces unmasked we look up to heaven
apologize for taking existence for granted
we shake hands again
look back on last spring with respect
realize we're all part of this

we've only been here an instant
and resisting our circumstance
is a fast track to disaster
I want you to answer
when I knock on the door of your conscious
when I ask if you stayed home
and took inventory of all the shit
collecting dust in your cupboards
that you never knew you didn't need
until the prospect of death
was sitting on your chest
grabbing hold of your lungs

this quarantine may be
the death of us
as we were
but we'll damn sure emerge
better

On This Day
March 1

the Lindenberg baby disappeared
to muddy footprints and ransom requests
4,000 miles away Jacques Leduc
was born in Brussels to become a composer
of eleven symphonies, two requiems,
twelve string quartets
on this day in D.C.
John F. Kennedy
established the peace corps
a woman in Cleveland Ohio
watched life escape
from her husband's lungs
across the sea, David Bowe
began penning a poem
that would later become
ashes to ashes
dust to dust
on this day
Mickey Mantle retired
a bomb exploded on Capitol Hill
and nobody died, but no one knew why
400,000 babies were born
the Luftwaffe was established
a statement was published
by the tobacco industry
promoting health and longevity
witch-hunts began
and women were hanged
on this day
Helen Keller said something
inspiring about heaven
Bobby Sands began a hunger strike
and lived two months before he died

on this day
a third of the world
is thought to cry
and two-thirds pray

Acknowledgements

Thank you to my mother, for showing me what it means to embody courage, fortitude, kindness, and patience. Who taught me what a feisty, independent woman looks like, and who has never once given up.

Thank you to my father, who taught me that men can be strong and vulnerable at once. Who has a soft spot a mile wide and a sense of humor that can always crack smiles.

Thank you to my brother, for igniting my competitive streak and teaching me the importance of silence.

Thank you to my amazing and wonderful friend Kiki for designing the art that graces these pages, for showing me how to be thoughtful, for encouraging creativity, and for your exceptional spirit. I am lucky to know you.

And finally, thank you to all the poets and writers who listened to my rough drafts, encouraged me at open mics, and created beautiful spaces for poetry to live and breathe. The WriteHouse community, Shout! The open mic, The Definitive Soap Box, and the medley of artists who call Southern California home.

I love each and every one of you, fully and endlessly. Thank you.

Past Publications

Past publications include *Barking Sycamores*, *If and Only If*, *Broadside*, and *Alchemy.* Sarah elf-published a book entitled *Surviving 23* in 2017, exploring her experience suffering from and overcoming and eating disorder. She has been featured on the Strong Runner Chicks blog, RunSpirited, and Moontide Press.

Made in the USA
Las Vegas, NV
18 December 2020